Gennaro Contaldo was born in Minori in Amalfi. He came to Britain in the late 1960s and worked in several restaurants around the country and in London, where he eventually opened the award-winning Passione. He came to public attention as the chef who inspired Jamie Oliver when they worked together at Antonio Carluccio's Neal Street restaurant. In spring 2011 he co-presented *Two Greedy Italians* on BBC2 with Antonio Carluccio and in spring 2012 a second series, *Two Greedy Italians Still Hungry*, was broadcast. He is the author of several cookbooks, including *Gennaro's Easy Italian*, *Gennaro's Italian Year*, *Gennaro's Italian Home Cooking* and *Passione*.

GENNARO

LET'S COOK ITALIAN

GENNARO

LET'S COOK ITALIAN

favourite family recipes

PAVILION

To my lovely family

First published in the United Kingdom in 2012 by
PAVILION BOOKS
10 Southcombe Street
London
W14 0RA

An imprint of Anova Books Company Ltd

Text © Gennaro Contaldo 2012
Design and layout © Anova Books 2012
Photography © David Loftus 2012

ISBN: 978-1-86205-953-5

Illustrations by Sara Mulvanny

A CIP catalogue record for this book is available from the British Library.
10 9 8 7 6 5 4 3 2 1
Repro by Mission Productions ltd, Hong Kong
Printed by Toppan Leefung Ltd, China

Cook's note: all eggs and vegetables are medium unless otherwise stated

CONTENTS

THE FAMILY THAT COOKS TOGETHER STAYS TOGETHER

Food brings people together. When I was growing up it was the favourite topic of conversation at the dinner table. This was the same table on which my mother would roll out fresh pasta, knead bread dough or bottle preserves. This table was our altar, a place where all members of our family sat to eat, discuss, argue, laugh, sometimes cry — we had the best of times around it. All my family cooked, including my father, who still liked to make his own meals when he was well into his 90s. My aunts, cousins, neighbours, friends, in fact everyone I knew, cooked — the meals weren't elaborate affairs, but this was good, honest family cooking.

When I first came to England in 1969 I found it odd that food was not a priority in people's lives — they mostly liked to grab a quick bite on the go or eat from a plate balanced on their laps. And, horror of horrors, pasta was out of a can! Of course, things have changed dramatically since then — the immigrants to this country have brought their national dishes and foods and we have been exposed to numerous cooking programmes on television, cookery books and magazines, enticing us to cook and experiment. More recently, with fears of GM foods and intensive farming, we have turned to organic, natural and seasonal produce. When I was young, we ate mainly locally grown food. Nowadays we can find all sorts of exotic things to eat, flown in from around the globe, but I still prefer to eat seasonally. I look forward to the first broad beans and peaches in summer, and some of my favourite produce in autumn — pears, walnuts and chestnuts.

As a parent, I strongly believe in implementing good eating habits from an early age, and showing my kids where our food comes from and how to cook it. I was taught to respect food; the chickens and rabbits we kept were treated humanely. We never wasted food and leftovers were always used. Now my girls really enjoy making bread, pizza, pasta or gnocchi with me, and baking cakes with their mum. They are fascinated to see what I bring home when I've been out hunting; they are not afraid to touch the game birds and aren't squeamish about watching me clean them. When I was old enough, my father would take me hunting – we only killed for food, never for fun – and he taught me a lot. My mother introduced me to wild herbs and mushrooms; I would go with her to the hills above our village of Minori and she would teach me to identify the different species. Food was all around us and dominated our lives. 'Cosa mangiamo per pranzo?' ('What shall we eat for lunch?') was a constant refrain.

Family life in Italy is changing. More women work outside the home, so they no longer have time to prepare fresh pasta and the other traditional dishes their mothers and grandmothers used to make. However, Italians still want to eat well, and even if their fresh pasta is shop-bought they will still try to ensure it's of good quality. Italians still talk about food a lot and, although their meals might be a little more rushed these days, the family still gets together for the evening meal around a table – and certainly always on Sundays.

It is so easy to buy everything ready-made these days that I think we forget we can actually make it ourselves. Take something as basic as bread; not only do my children and I have fun making the dough, watching it rise and enjoying that magical moment when it is baked, but I also know they are eating something good. For me, this is spending quality time with my family – and I am passing on some of my family traditions, which I hope will stay with them forever.

SOUP

We loved soup as children, especially during the colder months. My older sisters were the experts. They made soup with beans, pulses, vegetables and all sorts of leftovers — even stale bread. It was perfect comfort food, warming and gentle yet satisfying and full of goodness. We always kept different types of legumi (pulses) in small sacks — borlotti, cannellini, black-eyed, kidney and broad beans, peas and lentils. My sisters would patiently sift through them to discard any impurities and then soak them in cold water overnight before cooking them the next day with vegetables and herbs to make the most delicious, hearty soup. I dedicate this chapter to my elder sisters, Filomena, Genoveffa and Carmelina, for being the best soup-makers ever.

In rural Italy it was common for soup to be made early in the morning and left gently bubbling on the stove until everyone came home in the evening. This ensured an instant warm, home-cooked meal.

Soup is sometimes served instead of pasta or risotto as a primo (starter). For the evening meal, a light soup in the form of a vegetable or meat broth (usually chicken or beef) with small pastina shapes, and a good sprinkling of grated Parmesan is quite common. For a more substantial soup, small ravioli or bread dumplings are added. Pastina in brodo (small pasta shapes in broth) is an Italian favourite, and reminds me of home-cooking in my childhood.

Soups are easy to make, nutritious and economical, and they can be made in large quantities to be frozen and then enjoyed when you have little time to cook, making them nutritious 'fast food'. This is a perfect way to use up seasonal vegetables when you get a glut of, say, courgettes (zucchini), spinach or pumpkin.

I still enjoy soup at home today, and my wife Liz loves to make it — from light pastina broths for the girls and delicate vegetable puréed soups to substantial bean and pasta soups that are a meal in themselves.

Minestra di verdure

Vegetable soup

- - - - - - - - - - - - - - - - - - - -

SERVES 4–6

5 tbsp extra virgin olive oil

1 onion, finely chopped

1 garlic clove, finely chopped

40g/1^1/$_2$ oz pancetta or bacon, finely
chopped (optional)

2 potatoes, peeled and cubed

2 carrots, thickly sliced

1 celery stalk, thickly sliced

1 courgette (zucchini), cubed

1 leek, finely chopped

4 cherry tomatoes

100g/3^1/$_2$ oz podded fresh or frozen peas

100g/3^1/$_2$ oz podded fresh or frozen
broad (fava) beans

1.5 litres/2^1/$_2$ pints/1^1/$_2$ quarts vegetable stock

250g/9oz ditalini or other small pasta shape

salt and freshly ground black pepper

a few fresh basil leaves, finely chopped

Parmesan, grated, to serve (optional)

- - - - - - - - - - - - - - - - - - - -

There is nothing nicer at the end of a long day than a bowl of home-made vegetable soup. I usually throw in whatever fresh vegetables I have, plus frozen peas and broad (fava) beans, which I always keep (of course, in season, it is better to use these fresh, but if you do, add them with the rest of the vegetables at the beginning of the cooking, as they will require longer to cook.) The inclusion of small pasta shapes is to give the soup more bulk, but if you prefer a lighter soup, you can omit them.

Heat the extra virgin olive oil in a large saucepan, add the onion, garlic and pancetta, if using, and sweat, stirring, for 3 minutes. Add all the vegetables, (except the peas and broad beans if using frozen) and mix well. Add the stock and bring to the boil, then half-cover the pan with a lid, lower the heat and simmer gently for 30 minutes (adding the frozen peas and broad beans 10 minutes before the end of the cooking time).

Add the ditalini and cook until the pasta is al dente, following the cooking instructions on the packet. Remove from the heat, season to taste and stir in the basil leaves.

Serve immediately in individual bowls, with freshly grated Parmesan over the top, if desired.

Zuppa di borlotti e osso di prosciutto

Borlotti bean and prosciutto soup

SERVES 4

350g/12oz thick chunks of prosciutto, rinsed

2 large carrots, cut into chunks

2 onions, cut into chunks

2 celery stalks, cut into chunks

3 tomatoes, cut into chunks

2 bay leaves

a handful of fresh parsley, roughly chopped

20 black peppercorns

400g/14oz borlotti beans, cooked, drained and rinsed

55g/2oz Parmesan, grated

extra virgin olive oil, to drizzle

4 slices of country bread, grilled, to serve

In Italy no part of the pig is wasted and it is common to use even the prosciutto bone for soups and stews. The taste is really something else. If I can't get hold of a prosciutto bone, I use thick chunks of prosciutto (which you can ask for at delis) or a piece of gammon (ham). It is a delicious winter warmer and the slightly smoky smell of the prosciutto while cooking takes me back to family evening meals when I was a child. Nowadays, everything fatty seems to be prohibited, but when you make this dish, do include a little of the prosciutto fat – it will really enhance the flavour. If you are using dried borlotti beans, remember to soak them overnight and follow the cooking instructions on the packet. Alternatively, if you are in a hurry, the canned variety will suffice.

Put the prosciutto chunks, all the vegetables, the bay leaves, parsley, peppercorns and 2 litres/3^1/$_2$ pints/2 quarts water into a large pot. Place on a high heat and bring to the boil, then reduce the heat to medium, half-cover with a lid and cook for 1^1/$_2$ hours.

Add the borlotti beans and continue to cook for 10 minutes. Preheat the grill (broiler) to medium.

Remove the soup from the heat and divide it between 4 heatproof bowls, then sprinkle 1 tbsp of grated Parmesan on top of each. Place under the grill for a minute, until the cheese has melted slightly. Drizzle with extra virgin olive oil and serve immediately with country bread.

Zuppa di orzo e spinaci

Pearl barley and spinach soup

SERVES 4

200g/7oz pearl barley

4 tbsp extra virgin olive oil, plus extra to drizzle

60g/2¼oz bacon, roughly chopped

2 large potatoes, peeled and cut into chunks

1 garlic clove, peeled and left whole

4 cherry tomatoes, quartered

2 litres/3½ pints/2 quarts hot vegetable stock
(from powder or home-made)

200g/7oz spinach

freshly ground black pepper

Parmesan shavings, to serve

Pearl barley is typically used in soups in northern Italy. When I was growing up we used to have a drink known as orzata, which was made with this grain, but it was on a trip to Scotland during my early years in the UK that I came across it in soup. I have since added it to soups as an alternative to pasta or rice. With the addition of spinach, this is a nutritious and filling meal, which is especially welcome during the colder months.

Rinse the pearl barley in cold water and set aside.

Heat the extra virgin olive oil in a large saucepan, add the bacon, potatoes, garlic and tomatoes and sauté on a medium heat for 1 minute. Add the hot stock and bring to the boil, then reduce the heat to medium-low and simmer for 10 minutes.

Add the pearl barley, half-cover the pan with a lid and cook on a low heat for 1½ hours, until tender (check the instructions on the packet as they may vary). About 5 minutes before the end of the cooking time, add the spinach. Remove from the heat, season with black pepper and serve sprinkled with Parmesan shavings.

SERVES 4

1kg/2lb 4oz beef brisket

2 large onions, cut into chunks

2 celery stalks with leaves, cut into big chunks

2 large carrots, cut into big chunks

6 bay leaves

20 black peppercorns

a pinch of salt

200g/7oz pastina

Parmesan, grated, to serve

Pastina in brodo di carne

Beef broth with pastina

Pastina in brodo is comfort food and made by mothers all over Italy. It is light, warming and nourishing, suitable for young children, the elderly and convalescents. I suggest making extra broth to freeze in batches. There are many varieties of *pastina* – conchigliette (small shells), stelline (little stars), farfalline (small butterflies), pepe (peppercorns), alfabeto (alphabet) and tubettini (small tubes). My children have grown up on *pastina in brodo* and they love it; even the older ones still ask for it.

Place the beef, onions, celery, carrots, bay leaf, peppercorns and salt in a large pot with 2.5 litres/4$\frac{1}{2}$ pints/2$\frac{1}{2}$ quarts water and bring to the boil. Lower the heat, cover with a lid and simmer gently for 2–3 hours, until the meat is tender and falls apart. Skim off the fat, if necessary, during cooking.

Remove the meat and vegetables and set aside. Strain the liquid and pour back into the pan, then bring to the boil, add the *pastina* and cook as directed on the packet.

Remove from the heat and serve in individual bowls with grated Parmesan on top. You can serve the meat and vegetables as a main course if you wish.

SERVES 4

4 tbsp extra virgin olive oil, plus extra to drizzle

1 small onion, roughly chopped

600g/1lb 5oz courgettes (zucchini), thickly sliced

200g/7oz potatoes, peeled and cut into chunks

750ml/1 pint 6fl oz/3 cups vegetable stock

freshly ground black pepper

a handful of fresh basil leaves

30g/1oz Parmesan, grated

Zuppa di zucchine e basilico

Courgette and basil soup

This soup is simple to prepare and light and delicate in taste, with the freshness of courgettes (zucchini) and basil. Liz cooks it when my friend Paolo has a glut of courgettes in his allotment and she usually makes lots to freeze in batches. It is delicious for all the family, and was ideal when my girls were babies. Serve as a starter or with good bread as a light meal.

Heat the extra virgin olive oil in a medium saucepan, add the onion and courgettes and cook on a medium heat for about 5 minutes. Add the potatoes, stock and some black pepper, increase the heat and bring to the boil. Reduce the heat and simmer gently for 20 minutes.

Remove from the heat and stir in the basil, then blend until smooth. Stir in the Parmesan, heat through if necessary and serve drizzled with extra olive oil.

PASTA

PASTA

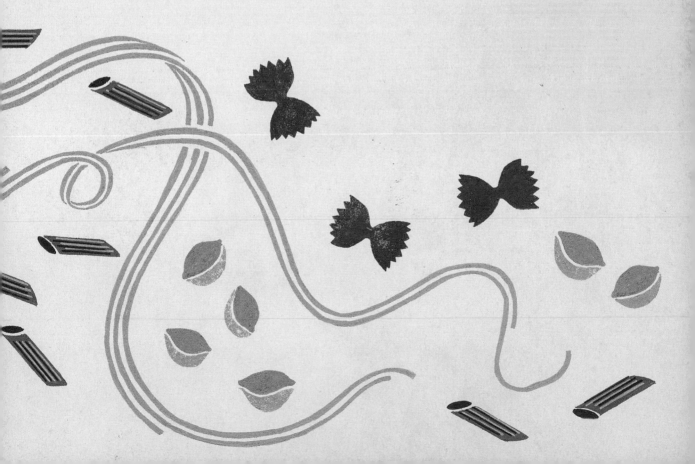

For most Italians a day would not be complete without a helping of pasta. When I was a child, my mother and Zia (Aunt) Maria would make fresh pasta at least once a week. It was usually eggless pasta, which is common in southern Italy, rather than the egg variety that is made in the north. They knew instinctively how much flour and water to use. This was always a happy time, as we children would gather round the long kitchen table to watch them roll out the dough and make different shapes. They chatted whilst working, and would tell us off for putting our fingers in the dough. They made the pasta by hand (machines were never used) and it was carefully but swiftly and expertly rolled with a rolling pin. They would use long, thin canes and umbrella spokes to make fusilli and ricci shapes and they made gnocchetti and orecchiette too.

We also had dried pasta, as it provided a quick and nutritious meal. But the ritual weekly pasta-making sessions are times I remember fondly and that pasta always tasted more special.

I still enjoy making pasta. I use a machine to roll out the dough and make shapes such as spaghetti and tagliatelle, while the children make nests with ribbons of pasta. I love to watch their faces as they do this – in between the odd argument as to whose turn it is to turn the handle or make the nests! I also make filled pasta, such as ravioli, tortellini, cappellacci, culurzones, panzerotti and mezzelune, by hand and, of course, the girls love to help.

My home village of Minori in southern Italy has a long tradition of pasta-making. Many small factories opened after the Second World War, employing locals to produce excellent dried pasta. I remember pasta hanging on long canes outside, left to dry in the sun, and the short shapes spread out on white sheets on the ground near the sea. The pasta was then packaged in blue recycled paper and sold. As the industry grew, these small factories closed down and were replaced by larger, famous-named factories in town and cities. But there is still a small family-owned shop in Minori run by my friend Antonio, who, together with his family, continues to make his own pasta and sell it to the locals.

Ladies from the older generation in Minori, like my great-aunt Antonietta, still get together, just like my mother and zia Maria did all those years ago, and make pasta. Entire afternoons are spent rolling, shaping, chatting, gossiping and producing great, genuine food. When I return home, I love to visit Zia Antonietta (now aged 90) and her friends and watch and admire. I fear this ritual will die away once these ladies are no longer with us, and that's why I like to show my daughters, in the hope they will keep the tradition alive.

Pasta is comfort food to me — it reminds me of home and I know I am eating a nutritious meal. When I felt a little down as a child, my mother would prepare a quick and simple pasta dish to perk me up and it really did the trick. Over the years, scientists have proved that pasta is highly beneficial in our diet — it's an excellent source of carbohydrate, releasing energy slowly, and contains serotonin, a feel-good substance. Although my mother was not a scientist, she knew what was good for me.

You can make pasta as rich or as light as you like, and to suit your budget. In Italy, the traditional family tends to serve it at lunchtime as a primo (starter), followed by a main course of meat or fish. However, it is perfectly acceptable to serve pasta as a main course with, say, a Bolognese ragù or vegetables, fish or pulses for a nutritious meal.

There are numerous pasta shapes — in the region of 600 — to choose from. When I am in Italy I love visiting the supermarkets to marvel at the varieties, all destined for different sauces and dishes. Italians insist that certain pasta shapes go with certain sauces, and they adhere to quite strict rules and regulations. For example, long pasta, such as spaghetti or bucatini, tends to marry well with quick-cook light sauces such as simple tomato or fish. Short shapes, such as penne and fusilli, go with heavier, more robust sauces such as a meat ragù. This is why Italian households usually dedicate a whole kitchen cupboard just to storing dried pasta. When I visit my sister Carmellina in Italy, the pasta packets tumble out of the cupboard as soon as someone opens it. She keeps a selection of long pasta such as spaghetti (which, incidentally, has varying sizes), tagliatelle, linguine and bucatini; short pasta such as penne, farfalle, fusilli and orecchiette; and tiny shapes for soup such as alphabet or stars, especially for her grandchildren — not forgetting lasagne sheets, cannelloni and paccheri for baked dishes made for special occasions. I like to keep a selection in my cupboard too, and I find a couple of varieties in each category is more than enough for our everyday family consumption.

Pasta fresca

Fresh pasta

- -

MAKES 300G/10^1/2OZ

200g/7oz/1^1/₃ cups '00' flour, plus extra to dust
2 eggs

- -

Fresh pasta can be made by hand simply with a rolling pin, like my mother, grandmothers and aunts did. However, I find it much easier and less time-consuming to use a pasta machine. They are available from kitchen shops and online. For home use, I suggest the small hand machine, but if you regularly make lots of pasta, then it is worth investing in the next size up. You can get electric machines, which mix the dough for you, but these tend to be costly and are very heavy.

Place the flour on a clean work surface or in a large bowl. Make a well in the middle and break in the eggs. Using a fork or your hands, gradually mix the flour with the eggs until combined. Knead for about 5 minutes to form a smooth, soft dough. Shape into a ball, wrap in clingfilm and leave for about 30 minutes, or until you are ready to cook.

Divide the pasta dough into 4 portions and roll each one through your pasta machine, starting at the highest setting. Continue to roll the pasta through the machine; as it gets thinner, turn down the settings until you get to number 1 and your pasta dough is almost wafer-thin.

Place the sheet of pasta on a lightly floured surface and use according to your recipe.

Non-egg fresh pasta

You can make pasta without eggs. Simply substitute 125ml/4fl oz/^{1}/2 cup hot (not boiling) water for the eggs and follow the method as above.

SERVES 4

1 tbsp extra virgin olive oil

30g/1oz/2 tbsp butter

1 small onion, finely chopped

40g/1¹/₂oz pancetta or bacon, finely chopped

250g/9oz podded fresh or frozen peas

6 fresh mint leaves (optional)

160ml/5¹/₂fl oz/generous ²/₃ cup hot vegetable stock

generous 1 tbsp freshly grated Parmesan, plus extra to serve (optional)

salt

300g/10¹/₂oz farfalle

Farfalle con pancetta e piselli

Farfalle pasta with pancetta and peas

This quick and easy recipe is especially favoured by my girls. I usually make it with frozen peas, but when in season, fresh peas are ideal – just cook them for a little longer and add a little extra liquid. Farfalle is a butterfly-shaped pasta that will particularly appeal to children.

Gently heat the extra virgin olive oil and butter together in a frying pan until the butter has melted. Increase the heat to medium, add the onion and pancetta and sweat until the onion has softened and the pancetta is golden. Stir in the peas and mint, if using, then add the hot stock and Parmesan, cover with a lid and cook on a medium heat for 3–4 minutes, until the peas are cooked and the water has been absorbed.

Meanwhile, bring a large saucepan of lightly salted water to the boil and cook the farfalle until al dente, according to the instructions on the packet. Drain, add to the sauce and mix well. Serve immediately with an extra sprinkling of Parmesan, if desired.

Orecchiette con zucca e broccoli

Orecchiette pasta with butternut squash and purple sprouting broccoli

- - - - - - - - - - - - - - - - - -

SERVES 4

3 tbsp extra virgin olive oil, plus extra to drizzle

1/2 red onion, finely chopped

1/2 garlic clove, finely chopped

85g/3oz pancetta or bacon, finely chopped

1 sprig of fresh thyme

1/2 red chilli (chile), finely chopped

250g/9oz butternut squash flesh, cut into cubes

salt

300g/10 1/2oz orecchiette

100g/3 1/2oz purple sprouting broccoli, stems trimmed, cut into chunks

30g/1oz Parmesan, grated, plus extra to sprinkle

a pinch of dried chilli (chile) (optional)

- - - - - - - - - - - - - - - - - -

Orecchiette, meaning 'little ears', are handmade eggless pasta shapes originating from Puglia and traditionally served with a sauce of broccoli and anchovies. It used to be quite usual to see women in this part of southern Italy sitting outside their homes making this pasta; it is still homemade in many households and my zia Antonietta is a 'professional'. As its popularity has grown, factories have begun producing orecchiette and it is now widely available, even here. I really like this type of pasta; it has quite a bite. This recipe uses butternut squash instead of anchovies, making it an excellent dish for all the family to enjoy. If you like a little heat, add some dried chilli (chile) at the end – it really enhances the squash. I love chilli, but usually just sprinkle it on for my wife Liz and me, and the children have it without.

Heat the extra virgin olive oil in a large frying pan, add the onion, garlic, pancetta, thyme and the fresh chilli and sauté for a couple of minutes. Add the pumpkin, and salt to taste, then lower the heat, cover the pan and cook for about 20 minutes, until tender. Add a couple of tablespoons of hot water if the pumpkin gets too dry.

Meanwhile, bring a large saucepan of lightly salted water to the boil and cook the orecchiette until al dente, according to the instructions on the packet. Drain and set aside.

Cook the broccoli in boiling water for about 5 minutes, until tender, then drain and stir into the cooked pumpkin. Add the drained orecchiette and grated Parmesan and mix well. Serve immediately with a drizzle of extra virgin olive oil, extra Parmesan and the dried chilli, if desired.

SERVES 4

4 tbsp extra virgin olive oil

1 garlic clove, squashed but left whole

250g/9oz canned good tuna steak,
drained

a handful of fresh parsley,
finely chopped

2 x 400g cans chopped plum tomatoes

salt and freshly ground black pepper

325g/11 1/2oz tripoline

Tripoline con tonno

Tripoline pasta with tuna

Tripoline is a long, ribbon pasta. It has a curly edge so that it can trap more sauce. It was one of my father's favourite types of pasta, and I remember him serving it with the season's first San Marzano tomatoes, which grew near where we lived, and raw garlic. The taste was unforgettable. I haven't recreated his recipe, as it is difficult to find these tomatoes in England. But roughly at the same time as the San Marzano tomato harvest, the tuna were in season. The boats would come into our small beach and this huge fish was on show for all to see. My mother would always buy a fair amount to preserve in oil, so I decided to combine the tripoline with this very simple store cupboard sauce of canned tuna and tomatoes. Quick and simple to prepare, it makes a nutritious meal for all the family.

Heat the extra virgin olive oil in a large frying pan over a high heat, add the garlic and sauté for 1 minute. Lower the heat to medium, discard the garlic and add the tuna and parsley. Cook for a couple of minutes. Add the tomatoes, salt and pepper and stir well, then cover with a lid and cook on a gentle heat for 20 minutes.

Meanwhile, bring a large saucepan of lightly salted water to the boil and cook the tripoline according to the instructions on the packet. Drain, then add to the sauce, mix well and serve.

SERVES 4

4 tbsp extra virgin olive oil
400g/14oz courgettes (zucchini), sliced
salt and freshly ground black pepper
325g/11^1/$_2$oz spaghetti
4 egg yolks
100ml/3^1/$_2$fl oz/^{1}/$_3$ cup milk
40g/1^1/$_2$oz Parmesan, grated, plus extra
to serve (optional)
a handful of fresh basil leaves, plus a
few to garnish

Spaghetti con zucchine alla carbonara

Spaghetti with courgette carbonara

This is based on the traditional carbonara recipe from Lazio, but I have replaced the *guanciale* (cured pork) with courgettes (zucchini) for a lighter version. I like making this dish as a quick, simple and nutritious midweek meal for the family. The addition of egg yolks is a great way of adding protein if the children are fussy eaters (but do not give raw or undercooked eggs to the very young).

Heat the extra virgin olive oil in a large frying pan, add the courgettes and stir-fry on a high heat until golden and cooked. Remove and drain, discarding the excess oil, then return to the frying pan and set aside.

Meanwhile, bring a large saucepan of lightly salted water to the boil and cook the spaghetti according to the instructions on the packet.

Whisk the egg yolks, milk, Parmesan and salt and pepper to taste in a bowl. Pour into the frying pan with the courgettes, and the basil leaves and heat through gently, stirring, until you have a creamy consistency. Remove from the heat.

Strain the spaghetti, reserving a little of the cooking water. Add the pasta to the sauce and mix well, pouring in a little of the cooking water, if necessary, to loosen the sauce. Garnish with a few basil leaves, sprinkle with grated Parmesan, if desired, and then serve immediately.

Bucatini alle melanzane

Bucatini with aubergine

- -

SERVES 4

175ml/6fl oz/$\frac{3}{4}$ cup extra virgin olive oil

400g/14oz aubergine (eggplant), cut into thin strips

2 garlic cloves, finely chopped

$\frac{1}{2}$ red chilli (chile), thinly sliced

a pinch of dried oregano

2 x 400g cans chopped plum tomatoes

a handful of fresh basil leaves, roughly chopped, plus extra to garnish

8 anchovy fillets in oil, drained

salt and freshly ground black pepper

350g/12oz bucatini

3 tbsp capers

85g/3oz pitted black olives, sliced

- -

This southern Italian dish has always been a family favourite and was usually cooked during summer. During this time of year we would be surrounded by aubergines and we would cook them in many dishes, as well as preserve them for our store cupboard. I remember my mother saying the best aubergine is the 'cime di viola', a long, thin, bright purple, seedless variety. When I see them here in the market I always buy them. Last year a friend had a glut of this variety in his allotment and gave me some – they had a really special taste. If you come across them during summer, I urge you to try them.

Heat 6 tbsp extra virgin olive oil in a large frying pan, add the aubergine and stir-fry on a medium heat for about 10 minutes, until golden-brown and cooked through. The oil will be absorbed quickly, but don't add more – when the aubergines are cooked the oil will exude from them. Remove, drain on kitchen towel and set aside.

Heat the remaining oil in the frying pan, add the garlic, chilli and oregano and sweat on a medium heat for 1 minute. Add the tomatoes and basil and cook for 15 minutes. Add the anchovies and cook for 5 minutes, stirring from time to time.

Meanwhile, bring a large saucepan of lightly salted water to the boil and cook the bucatini until al dente, according to the instructions on the packet. Drain and stir into the tomato sauce, then add the cooked aubergines and the capers and olives, toss well and serve immediately with a few fresh basil leaves.

Fusilli con datterini e olive taggiasche

Fusilli with baby vine tomatoes and taggiasca olives

This dish can be eaten warm or made in advance to enjoy cold as a salad – perfect for a family picnic! The kids will love the fusilli shape and, even if they are not keen on olives and onion, they will enjoy picking at the healthy tomatoes. If you can't find baby vine tomatoes, substitute cherry tomatoes. I love the unique taste of Ligurian taggiasca olives, which can be found in good Italian delis; but Kalamata olives make a fine substitute, and are widely available.

Combine the tomatoes, olives, onion, extra virgin olive oil and some salt and pepper in a large bowl, cover and set aside.

Bring a large saucepan of lightly salted water to the boil and cook the fusilli until al dente, according to the instructions on the packet. Drain well and add to the tomato mixture, tossing well. Scatter the basil leaves over and either serve immediately or enjoy cold as a pasta salad. Drizzle with a little extra virgin olive oil just before serving.

SERVES 4

4 tbsp extra virgin olive oil

$^1/_2$ onion, grated

1 small carrot, grated

$^1/_2$ courgette, grated

6 fresh basil leaves (optional)

500ml/18fl oz/generous 2 cups passata
(strained tomatoes)

2 tsp vegetable stock powder

salt and freshly ground black pepper

300g/10$^1/_2$oz penne

Parmesan, grated, to serve (optional)

Penne al pomodoro e verdurine

Penne with tomato and vegetables

This is my wife Liz's recipe, and she has made it for our daughters since they were very young. It's perfect for kids, and the vegetables can be blended into a smooth sauce if they prefer. You can make a lot and freeze it in batches, as we often do, for a quick, nutritious meal when you're pressed for time. Of course, it's delicious for grown-ups too!

Heat the extra virgin olive oil in a saucepan, add the grated vegetables and sweat on a medium heat for 3–4 minutes, until the onion has softened. Stir in the basil leaves, if you like, and the passata and powdered stock. Bring to a simmer, then reduce the heat to low, cover with a lid and cook for 25 minutes. Check for seasoning.

Meanwhile, bring a large saucepan of lightly salted water to the boil and cook the penne until al dente, according to the instructions on the packet. Drain, then add to the sauce and mix well. Serve immediately with grated Parmesan, if desired.

For older babies and toddlers

Omit the stock powder. Blend the sauce, once it's cooked, to a smooth purée. If you're doing this, there's no need to grate the vegetables, simply roughly chop, but remember to increase the cooking time for the larger pieces of vegetables.

Pasti Veloci

QUICK
MEALS

It's a shame that some people think a quick meal has to be shop-bought and ready-made, something you pop in the microwave. Of course it's much harder to cook from fresh these days, with most adults working and often facing a long commute home. Even in Italy, the land of the cooking mamma, people don't have time to prepare the two- or three-course meals their mothers used to make. However, ready-meals are expensive, and most contain high levels of fat, salt and sugar. And there is nothing nicer than sitting down to a home-cooked meal, whether it's a lavish affair or simply a bowl of pasta with home-made tomato sauce. It is nutritious, tasty and satisfying for all the family.

Pasta can be rustled up quickly, but there are other easy dishes that can be made in no time and that add variety to your diet. Risotto is the favourite in our house, and I use whatever ingredients we have: peas, courgettes (zucchini), carrots, broad (fava) beans, pumpkin; sometimes, if the fridge is bare, I serve it simply with butter and lots of Parmesan. Thinly sliced steak and scaloppine of veal, served with vegetables or salad, are also popular, and take little time to cook on the grill pan.

Chicken is quick to cook too, and if you get little pieces such as thighs, they can be roasted in a hot oven with small potato chunks, seasoned with garlic and rosemary, in less than half an hour; serve with steamed broccoli or green beans and you have a wonderful, nutritious meal with hardly any effort. Frittata is quick to make too, and a great source of protein. I add whatever is to hand, for instance cheese, prosciutto, pancetta, peas, courgettes and onions. I often make a big frittata and enjoy a slice the next day in a sandwich. Fish is also quick to cook, and one of the nicest ways to prepare it is to steam white fillets and drizzle them with extra virgin olive oil and lemon juice. Served with boiled baby potatoes, or mash for the kids, and green vegetables, this is a lovely healthy and light meal for everyone.

I believe with a well-stocked store cupboard and fridge, you can serve good, well-balanced, nutritious meals every day with a minimum of time and effort.

Risotto

Risotto is a predominately northern Italian dish, but we still enjoy eating rice in the south, and my mother would make her own version of risotto with lots of vegetables. The difference was in the cooking method – she would never stand by the pot stirring, as you should when making a traditional risotto. She would place rice, vegetables, some olive oil and lots of stock in a pot and let it bubble very gently until the rice was cooked and had absorbed all the liquid. She added olive oil and a little pecorino cheese at the end, but never butter and Parmesan. The result was less creamy than a normal risotto, but still very tasty.

I discovered 'real' risotto when I began working as a chef and travelled to northern Italian regions, where rice is cultivated. Here I learned that a number of types of rice work well in risotto (see page 62), as long as you use just one variety.

Like pasta, risotto in Italy tends to be served as a *primo* (starter) and can be combined with a variety of ingredients. It is often made with saffron (a traditional dish of Lombardy), mushrooms, or one of many vegetables, beans and pulses. It can be made simply, with butter and Parmesan or, for a lavish occasion, with shellfish and truffles.

I enjoy making risotto for the family – it's quick and nutritious and the favourite meal of my daughters Chloe and Olivia. I can guarantee clean plates when we've had risotto and it makes me happy to know they have eaten well. But they also enjoy getting involved and love to help with the stirring.

Risotto

Basic risotto

The first rule of risotto-making is to use the correct Italian rice – arborio, carnaroli or vialone nano. Do not use any other type, as the risotto will not work. Next, use good stock: home-made is ideal, but a good cube or powder will suffice. Your stock can be any type, depending on the ingredients in your risotto; for a basic risotto I use vegetable or chicken. Keep the stock gently simmering on the hob while you are adding it to the rice, as it must be added hot or the risotto will stop cooking. You may find you will need a little more or less than I have used in this recipe, as it will be affected by how you cook. Keep stirring the risotto or it may stick to the pan, and cook it gently on a low heat, making sure that all the liquid has been absorbed before you add the next ladleful. Once the risotto is cooked, the pan must be removed from the heat before you add the butter and Parmesan. If you follow these rules and stir for about 20 minutes, there is no reason why you shouldn't have a perfect risotto.

Put the stock in a saucepan and leave it gently simmering on a low heat.

Heat the extra virgin olive oil in a heavy-based saucepan. Add the onion and sweat on a medium heat until softened. Stir in the rice with a wooden spoon and coat each grain with the oil. Add a couple of ladles of hot stock and cook, stirring continuously, until the stock is absorbed. Add more stock and repeat. Continue adding stock, cooking and stirring in this way for about 20 minutes, until the rice is cooked. It should be soft on the outside but al dente on the inside.

Remove from the heat and, with a wooden spoon, beat in the butter and Parmesan until the ingredients are well combined and creamy. In Italy, this is known as *mantecare*. Check for seasoning and, if necessary, add salt and freshly ground black pepper. Serve immediately.

SERVES 4

1.5 litres/2½ pints/1½ quarts vegetable stock (from powder or home-made)
3 tbsp extra virgin olive oil
1 small onion, finely chopped
½ celery stalk, finely chopped
1 small carrot, finely chopped
1 bay leaf
200g/7oz minced (ground) pork
200g/7oz savoy cabbage heart, sliced
375g/13oz/scant 2 cups arborio rice
125ml/4fl oz/½ cup dry white wine
50g/1¾oz/4 tbsp butter
50g/1¾oz Parmesan, grated
salt and freshly ground black pepper

Risotto con carne macinata

Risotto with minced pork and savoy cabbage

This is a lovely way of using minced meat; it blends perfectly with risotto. This dish is a favourite quick and simple midweek meal in our house. I find pork mince very flavoursome, but you can use minced beef or a combination of the two.

Put the stock in a saucepan and leave it gently simmering on a low heat.

Heat the extra virgin olive oil in a medium, heavy-based saucepan. Add the onion, celery and carrot and sweat on a medium heat until softened. Add the bay leaf and mince, increase the heat to medium-high, and cook until the mince has browned all over. Add the cabbage, lower the heat

back to medium and cook, stirring, for 1 minute. Stir in the rice with a wooden spoon and coat each grain with the oil. Add a couple of ladles of hot stock and cook, stirring continuously, until the stock is absorbed. Add more stock and repeat. Continue adding stock, cooking and stirring in this way for about 20 minutes, until the rice is cooked. It should be soft on the outside but al dente on the inside.

Remove from the heat and, with a wooden spoon, beat in the butter and Parmesan until the ingredients are well combined and creamy. Check for seasoning and, if necessary, add salt and freshly ground black pepper. Serve immediately.

Bistecche alla pizzaiola

Steak in tomato sauce

This dish was a very popular quick meal in our household when I was a child. The tomato sauce was often served with pasta as a starter and then we would eat the meat afterwards. If you don't want pasta with it, serve it with lots of good bread to mop up the sauce.

Heat the extra virgin olive oil in a large shallow frying pan and fry the steaks for 1–2 minutes on each side to seal the meat. Remove and set aside.

Add the garlic, anchovies, capers and half the parsley and stir-fry for a couple of minutes. Add the tomatoes and oregano, stirring well, and cook on a high heat for 1 minute. Lower the heat, return the steaks to the pan, making sure they are covered with tomato sauce, and cook for 10–15 minutes, depending on the thickness of the meat. Check for seasoning and, if necessary, add salt and pepper. Remove from the heat, sprinkle on the remaining parsley and serve immediately.

SERVES 4

1kg/2lb 4oz chicken thighs and drumsticks
salt and freshly ground black pepper
a little plain (all-purpose) flour, to dust
150ml/5fl oz/²/₃ cup extra virgin olive oil
a bulb of garlic, cloves divided and skins left on
a large handful of fresh rosemary, broken in half
150ml/5fl oz/²/₃ cup dry white wine

for the bruschetta
a few slices of bread
a few garlic cloves, peeled

Pollo con aglio e rosmarino servito con bruschetta

Chicken with garlic, rosemary and bruschetta

This is a good old rustic chicken dish, full of flavour, which I love to make when I have friends round for a simple meal. It's easy to prepare, with just a few basic ingredients, and is made in just one large pan. This is exactly how we used to cook it at home at olive oil harvest time. Use good extra virgin olive oil, as you need quite a lot and the flavour of the dish is really enhanced by it. It's excellent served with the bruschetta.

Season the chicken with salt and pepper and dust with plain flour. Put the extra virgin olive oil in a large heavy-based frying pan and place on a medium-high heat. When hot, add the floured chicken and

seal well for 1–2 minutes on each side, until golden brown and quite crisp. Reduce the heat to medium-low, add the garlic and rosemary, cover with a lid and cook for 30 minutes, turning the chicken from time to time. Raise the heat to high, remove the lid, add the wine and simmer until it has evaporated. Check the chicken is cooked; the flesh should come away easily from the bone and there should be no sign of pink when you pierce the thickest part. Skim the oil from the top and set aside.

For the bruschetta, grill the bread, then immediately rub them with the garlic and drizzle with a little of the reserved oil. Serve the chicken with the bruschetta.

pasti a Lunga Cottura

SLOW
MEALS

When there is time, perhaps at the weekends or during holidays, I love to cook traditionally. It's good to slow down, know that I am not cooking in a restaurant kitchen or on a photo shoot, and recreate some of the dishes of my childhood. On cold days I cook huge pots of stew. Once the preparation has been done, I get on with other things or relax while the meat and vegetables gently bubble away on the stove and the cooking smells drift through the house. This is usually when one of the girls will notice and try to guess what's for dinner.

I love to eat anything made with beans or pulses – borlotti beans, cannellini beans, broad (fava) beans, peas, chickpeas, or green, red and brown lentils, as well as many others. They remind me of my childhood home in Italy, where they were a regular feature at dinner during the winter . Like my family, I use dried beans and pulses (but I do keep the odd can in my store cupboard for quick meals); I love soaking them in cold water the night before a meal in anticipation of what I might cook the next day, wondering what herbs and other ingredients we have available to flavour them with. Not only are beans and pulses very nutritious, fat-free and a good source of protein, they are also economical and delicious.

The girls love to help out in the kitchen, and we sometimes make gnocchi, fresh pasta or dough for bread and pizza together. They both adore sausages, so I showed them our simple family recipe for home-made sausages (see page 100) and now they want to make it all the time. Baked pasta and Parmigiana dishes are also favourites, and are good ways of using up leftover salami, cheese, tomato sauce and vegetables. They go a long way too – 1 large aubergine (eggplant) is more than enough to feed 4 people in a delicious and nourishing Parmigiana di melanzane. Filled and baked vegetables – (bell) peppers, courgettes (zucchini), onions or aubergines – are equally good; a mix of cheese, ham or salami and stale bread, or minced meat, will turn these humble vegetables into really filling and nutritious main meals.

Gnocchi di patate

Potato gnocchi

- - - - - - - - - - - - - - - - - - - -

SERVES 4–6

1kg/2lb 4oz floury potatoes such as King
Edwards, roughly all same size, scrubbed

salt

1 egg

300g/10$^{1}/_{2}$oz/generous 2 cups plain
(all-purpose) flour

rice flour, to dust

- - - - - - - - - - - - - - - - - - - -

Rice flour is better than plain flour for rolling out
gnocchi as it prevents the dough from sticking.

Put the unpeeled potatoes in a saucepan with lots
of cold water, bring to the boil and cook for 15–20
minutes, or until they are tender but not falling apart.
Drain, allow to cool slightly, then remove the skins.
While warm, mash the potatoes and leave to cool.

Place the mash in a large bowl, season with salt, stir
in the egg, add the flour and work to a soft dough.
Sprinkle the rice flour over a work surface and roll out
the dough into long sausage shapes. Using a sharp
knife, cut into 2cm/$^{3}/_{4}$ inch lengths. Set aside.

Bring a large saucepan of lightly salted water to the
boil. Drop the gnocchi into the water in batches and
simmer for a minute or so, until they rise to the top.
Remove with a slotted spoon and drain well, then
add to a sauce of your choice. Mix well and serve.

Zucchini ripieni al forno con salsa al pomodoro

Baked filled courgettes in tomato sauce

- -

SERVES 4–6

6 large courgettes (zucchini)
2 tbsp extra virgin olive oil
1 garlic clove, finely chopped
150g/5$\frac{1}{2}$oz minced (ground) beef
150g/5$\frac{1}{2}$oz minced (ground) pork
100g/3$\frac{1}{2}$oz stale white bread, soaked in a little water and squeezed
1 egg
30g/1oz Parmesan, grated, plus extra to sprinkle
a handful of fresh parsley, finely chopped
salt and freshly ground black pepper

for the tomato sauce
2 tbsp extra virgin olive oil
1 small onion, finely chopped
400g can chopped plum tomatoes

- -

It is common in Italy to stuff vegetables such as courgettes (zucchini). Traditionally this is done to enrich vegetables that are in season and make them into a substantial meal for the family. Typical leftovers of cheese, bread and salami are used, while minced (ground) meat and vegetarian fillings are common. This dish is the favourite comfort food of my partner, Liz, whose mum would often make it for her. Liz now makes this for the family and it is indeed yummy and satisfying.

For the sauce, heat the extra virgin olive oil in a pan, add the onion and sweat on a medium heat until softened. Add the tomatoes and season with salt and pepper, then reduce the heat to medium-low, half-cover with a lid and cook for 20 minutes, stirring from time to time.

Preheat the oven to 200°C/400°F/gas mark 6.

Cut the courgettes in half lengthways, scoop out the pulp and put the shells to one side. Heat the extra virgin olive oil in a frying pan, add the garlic and fry on a medium heat for 1 minute, then add the courgette pulp and stir-fry for about 4 minutes, until cooked. Leave to cool.

Combine the minced meats, bread, egg, Parmesan, parsley, cooked courgette pulp, salt and pepper in a bowl – this is best done with your hands. Fill the courgette shells with the mixture.

Pour the tomato sauce into an ovenproof baking dish. Place the filled courgettes on top, drizzle with a little extra virgin olive oil and sprinkle with Parmesan, then cover with foil and bake for 35 minutes. Remove the foil and bake for a further 10 minutes, until the courgettes are cooked through. If the tomato sauce has dried during baking, add a little hot water to the bottom of the dish. Remove from the oven, leave to stand for a couple of minutes, then serve.

Pranzo Domenicale

SUNDAY LUNCH

In Italy, Sunday is still considered an important day for religion, family and food. It's the one day when most people don't work and all the family reunites, usually around the dining table of mamma or nonna. When I was a child, it was the day you wore your 'Sunday best', and I suppose this is still true in smaller towns and villages. I love the atmosphere on Sunday in Italy — the church bells ring and, as Mass ends, the square fills with people, young and old, all immaculately dressed. Some go to the cafés for an aperitivo, some to buy pastries.

When I was a child, my parents, sisters, aunts, uncles and cousins would get together at my grandfather's house for Sunday lunch. He had a big table that would somehow accommodate all of us, up to 25 people. We would all contribute to lunch; my mother brought fresh pasta, my zia Maria meat ragù, and perhaps one of my sisters a dessert. If my father had been hunting, we'd have rabbit or quail, which he would prepare with my grandfather. It was always noisy, with the children laughing and playing, the dogs and cats waiting under the table for scraps, and the adults discussing the food — where it came from (my father's favourite topic), how a dish was cooked, and arguments about whether it should contain this herb or that. It was fun for me to get together with all my cousins, and now Sunday lunch brings back fond memories of family life in my childhood, and how food was a great part of it.

Sunday lunch might not be as noisy these days, and we might not consume as many courses as we did, but it's good to be together, cook together and share a roast or baked pasta dish. Sometimes my sister Adriana and her sons and my good friend Paolo (who is like one of the family) join us, or perhaps my elder daughter visits with her children, and then it does become noisy!

During the autumn, we often go to the forest to forage for mushrooms. The girls love it, and Olivia can spot a porcino before I do. When we have collected enough, we sometimes enjoy a mushroom risotto in the open; it's a special way of spending Sunday — with family, food and nature.

Il ragù di famiglia

My family's meat ragù

This has to be my favourite dish and is reminiscent of my childhood Sunday lunches. Traditionally, meat ragù was slow-cooked in terracotta pots for up to 12 hours. It may seem absurd, but believe me the taste was amazing. My zia Maria was the queen of ragù in our family and each week she would meticulously begin to prepare it the day before, leaving it to cook very gently until late at night, then recommence on Sunday morning, until all the family reunited at my grandfather's house. The tomato sauce was used to dress the home-made ricci pasta and the meat was served as a main course. This dish is still popular for Sunday lunch in most southern Italian families and I certainly like to make it when all the family comes to visit. Of course, the cooking time is greatly reduced. My sister Adriana recently gave me a tip to add chopped Parmesan to the sauce for even more flavour.

Heat the extra virgin olive oil in a saucepan, add the onion and bay leaves and sweat over a medium heat until the onion has softened slightly. Add the beef, ribs and sausages and fry for a few minutes, turning, to brown well.

Stir in the diluted tomato purée and allow to evaporate slightly. Add the tomatoes, salt, pepper, basil and Parmesan and stir well. Bring to the boil, then reduce the heat to low, cover with a lid and cook for 2 hours, checking and stirring from time to time.

Remove from the heat and serve as suggested in the introduction, with pasta or on its own with lots of good bread to mop up the tomato sauce.

Carre' d'agnello con carciofini

Rack of lamb with artichokes and sun-blushed tomatoes

4 large spring onions (scallions)
1kg/2lb 4oz rack of lamb
salt and freshly ground black pepper
85g/3oz prosciutto, roughly sliced
100ml/3^1/$_2$fl oz/^{1}/$_3$ cup extra virgin olive oil
leaves from 2 sprigs of fresh thyme
250g/9oz preserved artichoke hearts
250g/9oz sun-blushed tomatoes

This is a different way of cooking a roast rack of lamb – the flavours of the prosciutto, preserved artichokes and sun-blushed tomatoes really enhance the meat. It is simple to prepare and perfect to impress the family on a Sunday

Preheat the oven to 200°C/400°F/gas mark 6.

Cut the white parts off most of the spring onions and thinly slice them. Cut the remaining whole spring onions and green parts in half or into long slices, depending on their thickness.

Rub the rack of lamb all over with salt and pepper. Place the strips of prosciutto between the bones followed by the long spring onion slices and halves. Place in a roasting tin (pan) and drizzle with 4 tbsp extra virgin olive oil, rubbing it well in all over. Place in the oven for 30–40 minutes, or until cooked through.

Meanwhile, heat the remaining olive oil in a small pan, add the sliced white parts of the spring onions and sweat for a couple of minutes on a medium heat. Add the thyme, artichokes and tomatoes and cook for a further 2 minutes. About 10 minutes before the lamb is ready, add the vegetables to the roasting tin (pan) and return to the oven to finish cooking.

Zuppa inglese
Italian trifle

This is not an English soup, as the title suggests, but an Italian trifle. I am not sure where this recipe originates from, but it is suggested that the cooks of the Dukes of Este in Ferrara tried to recreate the English trifle after visits to England. The word *'zuppa'* (soup) in Italian cooking refers to both sweet and savoury dishes. The trifle is traditionally made with vanilla and chocolate *crema pasticciera* (custard) and *alchermes* (an aromatic, herb-infused, red-coloured liqueur); I have used Marsala, a traditional Sicilian fortified sweet wine, instead. If you can't find savoiardi biscuits, use sponge boudoir fingers. This recipe can be made the day before you plan to eat and stored in the fridge, and is a lovely family dessert for a Sunday lunch.

Put the milk in a jug, drop in the vanilla pod or lemon zest and leave to infuse. Meanwhile, whisk together the egg yolks and sugar for about 5 minutes, until the sugar has dissolved and the mixture is smooth and creamy. Add the flour and continue to whisk until well amalgamated. Strain the milk through a sieve, then whisk it into the egg mixture. Transfer to a pan and place on a low heat, stirring continuously, until it thickens. Pour half the custard into a bowl and add the cocoa powder, then whisk well, until amalgamated. Leave the 2 custards to cool.

Dip the savoiardi biscuits into the Marsala and use to line a serving bowl. Spoon in a layer of vanilla custard, then lay on more savoiardi biscuits, then chocolate custard. Continue layering, finishing with the chocolate custard, until you have used all the ingredients. Place in the fridge until required. Serve.

FESTE

SPECIAL OCCASIONS

SERVES 4

4 slices of Parma ham

4 slices of mortadella

4 slices of capocollo (cured
pork shoulder)

8 slices of Milano salame

250g/9oz buffalo mozzarella, roughly
sliced

a handful of green and black olives

a selection of preserved vegetables
such as (bell) peppers, aubergines
(eggplants), artichokes, sun-dried
tomatoes and mushrooms

grissini, bruschetta, focaccia and
country bread, to serve

Antipasto tradizionale

Classic antipasto

This classic Italian starter is traditionally served on special occasions such as Christmas. In rural Italy years ago every family had a pig, which was killed each year so that different cuts of cured meat would be available in the larder (pantry). The family also made numerous jars of preserved vegetables and their own cheese. All this produce would be carefully assembled to be enjoyed as an antipasto or starter. Nowadays, all you need is a trip to the supermarket or Italian deli to find these delicacies. Arrange them on big platters in the middle of the table and let everyone help themselves. Make sure you have plenty of good bread and grissini. You can also enhance this course by making some bruschetta (see page 132).

Arrange the meats, mozzarella, olives and preserves on a large platter. Serve with grissini, bruschetta, focaccia and country bread.

Porchetta

Stuffed rolled pork belly

- -

SERVES 10–12

5kg/11lb pork belly (ask your butcher to remove the ribs and trim the excess fat)

25g/1oz coarse sea salt

freshly ground coarse black pepper

small green leaves from a large handful of fresh thyme

leaves from a large handful of fresh rosemary, roughly chopped

a large handful of fresh sage leaves, roughly chopped

1 tbsp fennel seeds (if you are lucky enough to find wild fennel use it)

8 garlic cloves, finely chopped

2 tbsp extra virgin olive oil

potatoes, peeled and cut into chunks

small carrots, cut into chunks

6 tbsp runny honey

- -

Porchetta to me means a party and I make it during special occasions, when I know hordes of people will drop by. It feeds lots, can be eaten cold and can be stored in the fridge for up to a week. Traditionally in Italy, *porchetta* is a whole piglet filled with lots of fresh herbs and slow-roasted either in a wood oven or even outdoors on a spit. It is made at home, as well as sold ready-made as a takeaway. Since whole piglets are not that easily obtainable, I use pork belly and the result is similar. It is simple to prepare and can be made in advance and eaten cold – a great idea for large gatherings. It's ideal served with preserved vegetables such as Giardiniera (see page 224) and Preserved aubergines (see page 226).

Preheat the oven to 220°C/425°F/Gas 7. Lay the pork belly flat, skin side down. Sprinkle with half the salt and lots of black pepper, rubbing it well into the meat with your fingers. Leave to rest for 10 minutes so that the seasoning settles well into the meat. Sprinkle the herbs, fennel seeds and garlic evenly all over.

You will need 10 pieces of string, each about 30cm/12 inches long. Carefully roll the meat up widthways and tie it very tightly with string in the middle of the joint. Then tie at either end about 1cm/1/2 inch from the edge and keep tying along the joint until you have used up all the string. The filling should be well wrapped – if any escapes from the sides, push it in. Using your hands, massage 1 tbsp extra virgin olive oil over the joint, then rub in the remaining salt and some more black pepper.

Grease a large roasting pan with the remaining olive oil and place the pork in it. Roast for 10 minutes, then turn it over. After 15 minutes, reduce the oven temperature to 150°C/300°F/gas mark 2 and cover the pork with foil (if you like the crackling to be very crispy, don't bother with the foil, but remember the *porchetta* needs to be thinly sliced and crispy crackling will make that difficult). Roast for 3 hours.

If cooking the potatoes and carrots, add them to the roasting dish for the final 1 1/2 hours of cooking.

Remove the joint from the oven and coat with the honey, drizzling some of the juices from the roasting tin over it too. Insert a fork at either side of the joint and lift onto a wooden board. Leave to rest for 5 minutes, then slice and serve hot or cold.

Fritto misto di pesce

Mixed fried fish

- - - - - - - - - - - - - - - - - - - -

SERVES 4

200g/7oz king prawns (jumbo shrimp)

200g/7oz whitebait

200g/7oz squid (calamari), cleaned
and cut into rings and tentacles

200g/7oz sardines, gutted

grated zest of 2 unwaxed lemons

1 small garlic clove, finely chopped

a handful of fresh parsley, finely chopped

good vegetable or seed oil, to deep-fry

lemon wedges, to serve

for the batter

2 egg yolks

a pinch of salt

200g/7oz/1⅓ cups plain
(all-purpose) flour, sifted

- - - - - - - - - - - - - - - - - - - -

This dish was commonly served during the Christmas Eve feast, when meat was not permitted and the meal consisted of fish and vegetables. A large platter of *fritto misto* was placed in the middle of the table and everyone helped themselves. *Fritto misto* is also popular in restaurants at coastal resorts throughout Italy. The traditional way of making this dish was to simply dust the fish with flour and then fry them. I like a light batter, which works really well with the delicate flavour of the fish. The secret of this recipe is to use really fresh fish.

Place the prawns, whitebait, squid and sardines in a shallow dish and scatter half the lemon zest and all the garlic and parsley over them. Cover and refrigerate for 30 minutes.

To make the batter, whisk the egg yolks in a bowl, then gradually whisk in 40ml/1½fl oz/scant 3 tbsp very cold water and the salt. Gradually fold in the flour, until well amalgamated.

Heat the oil for deep-frying in a large saucepan or deep-fryer until a small piece of bread dropped in sizzles immediately. Remove the fish from the fridge and dip each piece into the batter, then immediately fry a few pieces at a time for a few minutes, until golden and the fish is cooked. Drain on kitchen towel and serve immediately, scattered with the remaining lemon zest, with lemon wedges.

Contorni

ON
THE SIDE

Broccoli con aglio, olio e peperoncino

Sautéed long stem broccoli with garlic and chilli

Broccoli is such a nutritious vegetable and I especially like the long-stem or purple sprouting variety. I love it with lots of chilli (chile) and garlic, but for the children I add less chilli or omit it altogether. This makes a lovely accompaniment to sausages and other meat dishes, or can be enjoyed with bread as a light meal.

Heat the extra virgin olive oil in a frying pan, add the garlic and chilli and sweat for 1 minute on a medium–high heat. Add the broccoli and some salt and pepper and stir-fry for 1 minute. Add 150ml/5fl oz/$^2/_3$ cup water, reduce the heat to medium, cover with a lid and cook for about 10 minutes, until tender.

Remove the lid, increase the heat and allow the liquid to evaporate. Remove from the heat, pour in the lemon juice, if using, and serve.

Insalata di pane bagnato

Bread salad

SERVES 4

3 tbsp red wine vinegar

4 slices of good country bread, about 1cm/$\frac{1}{2}$ inch thick

1 garlic clove, peeled

4 firm plum tomatoes, sliced

1 red onion, thinly sliced

1 small yellow (bell) pepper, deseeded and cut into strips

85g/3oz cucumber, thinly sliced

2 celery stalks with leaves, thinly sliced

a handful of fresh basil leaves

6 tbsp extra virgin olive oil, plus extra to drizzle

salt and freshly ground black pepper

a pinch of dried oregano

This recipe has peasant origins. During the warmer season in areas of southern and central Italy, farmers would wet pieces of stale bread with home-made vinegar and eat them with whatever produce was available in the fields – tomatoes, cucumber, peppers. This makes a lovely, light meal and is very healthy. The vinegar really enhances the salad and makes you want to eat more. My daughter Olivia loves vinegar and raw crunchy vegetables, so why not try it out on your children for a healthy lunch? I'm sure they'll be impressed with all the wonderful colours of the salad and, of course, you can substitute other vegetables, depending on what you and your family prefer.

Dilute the vinegar with 4 tbsp water. Place a slice of bread on each serving plate. Rub the bread with garlic and drizzle with the vinegar mixture.

Place the sliced tomatoes, onion, pepper, cucumber, celery and basil leaves in a bowl, add the extra virgin olive oil, season with the salt, pepper and oregano and toss well.

Divide the salad between the slices of bread and leave to rest for about 10 minutes. Drizzle with extra virgin olive oil and serve.

There is an old Italian saying, 'Buono come il pane' (literally 'as good as bread'), when talking about a good person because that is exactly what bread is. For me, bread is everything. When you have it, you need little else. It is healthy, nutritious and feeds the soul. In Italy it is served at each meal and bought fresh each day from the panetteria (bakery).

The smell of freshly baked bread evokes warm feelings of home and family. My mother used to make it every Thursday. It was a ritual; she would light the wood-fired oven the night before and wake up extra early the next morning to stoke the fire. As the loaves baked, the smell would slowly waft through the house and immediately had me out of bed and into the kitchen. A few cooked loaves would be on the kitchen table, others still in the oven. She would often add sugar and perhaps some dried fruit and citrus zest to the remaining dough to make a pane dolce (sweet bread, see page 195). I loved to tear the first loaf apart and eat the warm bread – the taste was heavenly.

Long after we had all left the family home, my mother would make bread when we went to visit. In those early days, when I travelled to and from Italy by train, she would often enrich it with ham, salami and cheese, and give it to me for the journey back. Being a young man, I didn't really want to have a knapsack, but she always insisted and I was so glad, because on that long, melancholic journey through France during the night, when I felt lonely and hungry, the taste of my mother's bread and the memories of home it evoked soon filled me with warmth and happiness.

Bread means tradition. It is made all over the world, in different ways, but the basic ingredients are the same. In Italy it is never thrown away – that would be a sin, and old wives' tales said that if you did, bad luck would be bestowed upon you. Bread was thought to be holy food and a gift from God. Leftover, stale bread was always used up, for breadcrumbs, in panzanella (bread salad), as fillings, or put back in the oven to double-bake as a hard biscuit-type bread.

MAKES 2 LARGE PIZZAS

1 quantity of pizza dough (see page 183)
dried breadcrumbs, flour or semolina, to dust

for the topping
3 tbsp extra virgin olive oil, plus extra, to drizzle
1 garlic clove, finely chopped
1/2 red chilli (optional), roughly chopped
250g/9oz tender-stem broccoli, stems trimmed
250g/9oz pork sausages, roughly chopped
(skinless, if preferred)
salt and freshly ground black pepper, to taste
400g can chopped plum tomatoes

La pizza di Olivia

Olivia's pizza

Olivia's favourite food is pizza, but she really enjoys sausages and broccoli too, so we combined them together. (Sausages with broccoli is actually a very common dish in southern Italy; the broccoli used is the *cime di rapa* (rape tops), slightly bitter-tasting with lots of leaves, which are also cooked.) This pizza is highly nutritious and filling, and really a meal on its own.

Make the pizza dough as described on page 183.

Preheat the oven to its highest setting.

Heat the extra virgin olive oil in a large frying pan, add the garlic and chilli, if using, and sweat on a medium-high heat for a couple of minutes. Add the broccoli, sausage and salt to taste and sauté for 1 minute. Cover with a lid, reduce the heat to medium and cook for 15 minutes.

Meanwhile, prepare the bases. Sprinkle a little flour on a clean work surface and, using your fingers, spread a piece of dough into a circle roughly 28–30cm/11–12 inches in diameter. The dough must be very thin, but be careful not to tear it. Repeat with the other ball of dough. Sprinkle some breadcrumbs, flour or semolina over 2 large flat baking sheets and place the pizza bases on them.

Remove the sausage and broccoli from the heat. Put the tomatoes in a bowl, season with salt and pepper and a drizzle of extra virgin olive oil, and stir. Spoon the tomatoes over the pizza bases, then scatter with the sausages and broccoli and drizzle with extra virgin olive oil. Reduce the oven to 220°C/425°F/gas mark 7 and bake the pizzas for about 8 minutes, or until cooked.

La pizza di Chloe

Chloe's pizza

- -

MAKES 2 LARGE PIZZAS

10g/¼oz fresh yeast or 1 x 7g sachet of dried
325ml/11fl oz/scant 1½ cups lukewarm water
500g/1lb 2oz/3½ cups strong plain (all-purpose
bread) flour, plus extra to dust
2 tsp salt
dried breadcrumbs, flour or semolina, to dust
400g can chopped plum tomatoes, optional

for the topping
extra virgin olive oil, to drizzle
2 balls of mozzarella, roughly chopped
6 slices of Parma ham, roughly torn

- -

The topping on this pizza includes Chloe's favourite ingredients. This type of *pizza bianca* is not traditional, but has become popular in *pizzerie* all over Italy during the last 20 years.

Dissolve the fresh yeast in the water (if you are using easy-blend/active dry yeast, just mix it in with the flour). Combine the flour and salt for the dough in a large bowl, then gradually add the dissolved yeast liquid (or dried yeast and water), mixing well to form a dough. Shape the dough into a ball, cover with a cloth and leave to rest for 5 minutes.

Knead the dough for 10 minutes, until smooth and elastic, then split in half. Knead each piece for 2 minutes, then shape into a ball. Sprinkle some flour on a clean tea towel or baking sheet and place the dough on it. Cover with a slightly damp cloth and leave to rise in a warm place for at least 1 hour.

Preheat the oven to its highest setting.

Sprinkle a little flour on a clean work surface and, using your fingers, spread a piece of dough into a circle roughly 28–30cm/11–12 inches in diameter. The dough must be very thin, but be careful not to tear it. Repeat with the other ball of dough. Sprinkle some breadcrumbs, flour or semolina over 2 large flat baking sheets and place the pizza bases on them.

If using the tomatoes, put them in a bowl, season with salt and pepper and a drizzle of extra virgin olive oil, and stir. Spoon the tomatoes over the pizza bases (if not using tomatoes, just drizzle the bases with extra virgin olive oil). Arrange the mozzarella pieces on top, followed by the Parma ham. Reduce the oven temperature to 220°C/425°F/gas mark 7 and bake the pizzas for about 8 minutes, or until cooked. Remove from the oven, top with the rocket and drizzle with some more extra virgin olive oil.

Sformato di pane alle verdure

Italian vegetable pie

- - - - - - - - - - - - - - - - -

SERVES 6–8

1 x 7g sachet of dried yeast

150ml/5fl oz/^{2}/$_3$ cup lukewarm water

250g/9oz/1^2/$_3$ cups '00' flour or strong plain
(all-purpose bread) flour, plus extra to dust

25g/1oz/2 tbsp softened butter, cut
into pieces

for the filling

3 tbsp extra virgin olive oil, plus extra to brush
and drizzle

500g/1lb 2oz potatoes

salt and freshly ground black pepper

1 small onion, thinly sliced

300g/10^1/$_2$oz courgettes (zucchini), thinly sliced

4 artichokes preserved in oil, sliced
(reserve 2 tbsp of the oil)

600g/1lb 5oz spinach

2 eggs

50g/1^3/$_4$oz Parmesan, grated

- - - - - - - - - - - - - - - - -

Pies are not normally associated with Italian cooking, but in Campania it is traditional to make a savoury pie during Christmas. It is made with leftover bread dough enriched with lard and escarole, mixed with anchovies, capers, pine kernels and olives. The pie is a nutritious snack, which farmers used to take with them to the fields for lunch, and I remember finding a slice in my school lunchbox – a treat my nonna (grandmother) would put in, as she made the pie for my nonno (grandfather), who loved it. I have made a lighter version – and believe me, once you start on a slice, you will want more.

Dissolve the yeast in the water. Combine the flour, butter and a pinch of salt in a large bowl. Make a well in the centre, gradually pour in the yeasted water and mix well to form a soft but not sticky dough. Knead on a lightly floured surface for 10 minutes, then form into a ball, cover with a clean tea towel and leave to rise in a warm place for 2 hours.

Preheat the oven to 200°C/400°F/gas mark 6. Lightly grease a baking sheet with olive oil.

Peel the potatoes and slice into rounds about 5mm/^{1}/$_4$ inch thick. Place on the baking sheet, sprinkle with salt and pepper and drizzle with extra virgin olive oil. Roast for about 15 minutes, until cooked through but firm.

Meanwhile, heat 3 tbsp extra virgin olive oil in a frying pan, add the onion, then sweat over a medium heat until it has softened. Add the courgettes and sauté on a medium heat for 10 minutes until softened. Add the artichokes with their oil and cook for 5 minutes. Add the spinach and salt and pepper to taste, cover with a lid and cook for 5 minutes. Allow to cool.

Increase the oven temperature to 220°C/425°F/ gas mark 7. Beat the eggs in a bowl, then stir in the Parmesan and some salt and pepper. Add the cooled vegetables and gently combine.

Line a round 23cm/9 inch diameter pie dish with greaseproof paper. Divide the dough in half. Roll out one half on a lightly floured surface and line the bottom and sides of the pie dish. Arrange the cooked potatoes on the bottom, followed by the vegetable filling. Roll out the other piece of dough and cover the pie, sealing well so that the filling does not escape. Prick all over with a fork and brush with extra virgin olive oil. Bake in the oven for 30–35 minutes, until golden. Can be eaten hot or cold.

When I was a child, dessert was usually fresh fruit. As soon as the main course was over, my mother would put the fruit bowl on the table so we could help ourselves. I loved picking cherries, peaches, apricots, wild strawberries and, my favourite at the end of summer, figs. I always knew where the best fruit was and which tree had the ripest — I checked daily. When I brought home lots of fruit, my mother would transform it into jams, cakes and crostate (tarts), which I would enjoy for merenda (afternoon snack). If I picked morello cherries she would put them in jars with sugar and leave them in the sun for a few days, until the sugar had dissolved and a wonderful cherry syrup was left, which would be used in ice cream and pasticiotto (a type of cherry pie).

Most desserts, cakes and biscuits were made at home by women. My grandmother's speciality was apple cake, my mother's was fruit tart and my sisters would experiment with biscuits, fruit salads and ice cream. Sweet treats were usually made from leftovers — bread dough was used to make pan dolce or sweet pies and a glut of fruit would go into tarts and cakes. We also enjoyed ricotta as a dessert; this was freshly made and sometimes served warm with a little sugar or cinnamon sprinkled over the top. A lot of southern Italian cakes and pastries include ricotta — for instance the Sicilian cassata (see page 214) and cannoli (little filled tubes of pastry dough), as well as tarts and cakes.

There was a small pasticcieria in our village of Minori, and sometimes, usually for a special occasion, we would buy cakes there. We knew the family who owned it and now and then I helped with odd jobs such as skinning almonds (not the most glamorous of tasks); it was interesting to watch the pasticciere (pastry chef) at work. The pasticcieria has grown considerably since I left and is now quite a famous spot to enjoy their lemon cakes. I love desserts and have a very sweet tooth; I don't have much time to make them these days, but when I do I tend to recreate my mother's fruit crostate (see page 210).

Gelatina di vino bianco con frutti di bosco

White wine jelly with fruits of the forest and strawberry sauce

SERVES 4

1 leaf or sheet of gelatine
200ml/7fl oz/scant 1 cup dry white wine
70g/2^1/$_2$oz/^{1}/$_3$ cup caster (superfine) sugar
^{1}/$_2$ clove
1cm/^{1}/$_2$ inch piece of cinnamon stick
25g/1oz raspberries
25g/1oz blueberries
4 fresh mint leaves, plus extra to decorate
4 tsp good natural yogurt

for the strawberry sauce

100g/3^1/$_2$oz strawberries, hulled,
plus extra, sliced, to decorate
juice of ^{1}/$_2$ lemon
2 tbsp caster (superfine) sugar

Jelly (jello) in desserts is not traditionally Italian, but it has become popular in restaurants and at home, particularly for children's parties. I like this recipe for summer entertaining, to make use of the season's berries. It looks stunning served in small liqueur glasses. Because of the alcohol content, the portions are small. For children, substitute freshly squeezed orange or elderflower juice for the wine.

Place the gelatine in a bowl of cold water to soften. Meanwhile, combine the wine, sugar, clove and cinnamon stick in a small saucepan and place over a medium heat. Bring to the boil, then boil rapidly for 3 minutes, until the sugar has dissolved. Remove from the heat and remove and discard the clove and cinnamon. Drain the gelatine, squeeze out the excess water, then stir the gelatine into the liquid and leave to cool.

Meanwhile, blend all the ingredients for the sauce to a smooth consistency in a food processor, then cover and refrigerate.

Divide the cooled jelly liquid between 4 x 100ml/3^1/$_2$fl oz liqueur glasses, filling them to just over halfway. Drop a few raspberries, blueberries and a mint leaf in each glass. Place in the fridge for 6 hours, or until the jelly has set. When set, top the jellies with the strawberry sauce, then a dollop of yogurt, and decorate with strawberry slices and mint leaves. Cover and store in the fridge until required.

SERVES 4–6

2 peaches, pitted

2 white peaches, pitted

4 apricots, pitted

4 kiwi fruit, peeled

200g/7oz strawberries, hulled

100g/3^1/$_2$oz blueberries

100g/3^1/$_2$oz/^{1}/$_2$ cup caster
(superfine) sugar

juice of ^{1}/$_2$ lemon

juice of 1 large orange

a few fresh mint leaves, to decorate

Macedonia estiva

Summer fruit salad

For me, fruit is the best dessert, and what better way to celebrate summer than by putting all the season's fruits together. *Macedonia* (fruit salad) has always been popular in Italy. Different fruits are used depending on the season, but sugar and citrus fruits are typically used for the dressing. Once the fruit has been left to macerate, a lovely sweet syrup develops and enhances the taste of the fruit. This simple summer dessert is delicious served with lemon sorbet (sherbet), if desired, and can be enjoyed by all the family or when entertaining. Easy, nutritious and packed with vitamins, it makes a refreshing end to a meal.

Slice the peaches, white peaches, apricots, kiwi fruit and strawberries and place in a large bowl with the blueberries.

Combine the sugar with the lemon and orange juices in a small bowl and mix well until the sugar has dissolved. Pour over the fruit, decorate with mint leaves, cover and allow to macerate for at least 30 minutes before serving.

Il gelato della nonna Fausta

Nonna Fausta's ice cream

- -

SERVES 4

2 egg yolks
250g/9oz/1¹/₄ cups caster (superfine) sugar
500ml/18fl oz/generous 2 cups milk
6cm/2¹/₂ inch vanilla pod (bean), split
6 slices of unwaxed lemon peel
biscuits such as savoiardi, to serve

- -

This recipe comes from my wife Liz's grandmother, who used to make it for her during the annual summer visit to Italy. Two aluminium trays of it were always in the freezer: one vanilla and one chocolate. This is the traditional way of making ice cream and, according to Nonna Fausta, the secret is getting the sugar content right. When I recreated this recipe, it took me back to my childhood days and my immediate reaction was *'sapore genuino'* ('it has the genuine taste!').

Beat together the egg yolks and sugar until creamy. Add the milk and whisk well. Add the vanilla pod and lemon peel. Pour into a saucepan, place over a gentle heat, stirring well all the time, until almost boiling. Remove from the heat and leave to cool, then remove the vanilla pod and lemon peel.

Place in a plastic container and freeze for 6 hours, removing from the freezer every 20 minutes to stir gently but thoroughly. Continue to do this for about 6 hours. (Alternatively, once your cream has cooled, place in the ice-cream maker and follow the instructions, then put in the freezer.)

Serve the ice cream in scoops in glasses with savoiardi biscuits.

For chocolate ice cream

To make a chocolate ice cream, make as above, but omit the vanilla and lemon peel. When you remove the pan from the heat, gradually add 25g/1oz good sifted unsweetened cocoa powder, whisking well to avoid lumps. Then proceed with the freezing process by hand or machine.

SERVES 6

175g/6oz/1¼ cups plain (all-purpose) flour, plus extra to dust

75g/2¾oz/6 tbsp cold butter, plus extra to grease

75g/2¾oz/⅓ cup caster (superfine) sugar

finely grated zest of 1 unwaxed lemon

2 egg yolks

1 x 250ml/9fl oz/generous 1 cup of strawberry jam (see page 232)

1 egg, beaten

icing (confectioner's) sugar, sifted, to dust

Crostata di Mamma

My mum's jam tart

Simple homemade jam or fruit tarts like this one are common all over Italy, made by mammas for their children, usually for *merenda* (teatime). My mum used to make this tart for us, filled with her delicious strawberry jam. The pastry is simple to make and, if you make a large quantity, it can be frozen to use later. By preparing your own pastry and filling, you can create a simple and nutritious sweet treat.

To make the pastry, put the flour on a clean work surface and rub in the butter until the mixture resembles breadcrumbs. Add the sugar, lemon zest and egg yolks and mix well to form a smooth dough. Shape into a ball, wrap in clingfilm (plastic wrap) and leave in the fridge for 30 minutes, or until required.

Preheat the oven to 180°C/350°F/gas mark 4. Grease a round 20cm/8 inch tart tin (pan) with a little butter.

Roll out the pastry on a lightly floured surface and use to line the greased tart tin. Cut off the trimmings and form them into a ball, then roll out and cut into 12 strips.

Fill the pastry case with the jam, then arrange the strips over the tart in a lattice pattern. Brush the strips with the beaten egg, then bake the tart for 25 minutes, until lightly golden.

Leave to cool slightly, then sprinkle with icing sugar and serve.

MAKES 25–30 BISCUITS

250g/9oz fine polenta (cornmeal)

100g/3^{1}/$_{2}$oz/^{2}/$_{3}$ cup cornflour (cornstarch)

175g/6oz/generous ^{3}/$_{4}$ cup caster (superfine) sugar

finely grated zest of 1 orange

finely grated zest of 1 unwaxed lemon

175g/6oz/generous ^{3}/$_{4}$ cup butter, melted

2 eggs, beaten

Biscotti di polenta agli agrumi

Citrus polenta biscuits

Using polenta (cornmeal) in desserts has become fashionable, and it is often made into cakes and biscuits. Apart from being delicious, with that extra crunch that polenta flour gives, these biscuits are a perfect sweet treat for anyone suffering from wheat intolerance. Simple to make and quick to bake, they are an ideal accompaniment to ice cream (see Il gelato della nonna Fausta, page 204) or to enjoy with a cup of tea. Space them well apart on the baking tray, as they spread during cooking; if necessary, bake in batches.

Preheat the oven to 180°C/350°F/gas mark 4. Combine the polenta, cornflour, sugar and orange and lemon zests in a bowl. Make a well in the centre, pour in the melted butter and beaten eggs and stir well. Cover and refrigerate for 20 minutes, until it becomes a little firmer.

Line 2 large baking trays with non-stick greaseproof paper. Place ^{1}/$_{2}$ tbsp dollops on the paper, spacing them at least 6cm/2^{1}/$_{2}$ inch apart. Bake for 12 minutes, until the edges turn golden. Leave to cool slightly before serving.

Torta di mela di Nonna Genoveffa

Granny Genoveffa's apple cake

SERVES 4–6

85g/3oz/6 tbsp unsalted softened butter, plus extra to grease

3 Granny Smith apples

juice and finely grated zest of 1 small unwaxed lemon

3 eggs

150g/5½oz/¾ cup caster (superfine) sugar

1 vanilla pod

300g/10½oz/generous 2 cups self-raising (self-rising) flour

This is a homely cake that, while baking, fills the house with a wonderful aroma. In the fall I would bring home basketfuls of apples and always made sure I gave lots to my grandma because I knew she would make this cake. She would bake several to give to family and friends. I gave the recipe to my wife Liz, who now makes it, and I can't tell you how quickly the slices disappear, often still warm. I have used Granny Smith apples, but any will suffice and if you prefer you can substitute pears, plums or apricots – a cake for every season.

Preheat the oven to 180°C/350°F/gas mark 4. Grease a round, 20cm/8 inch diameter, loose-bottomed cake tin (pan) with a little butter, then line with non-stick greaseproof paper.

Peel and core the apples, chop them into medium chunks and put them in a bowl. Squeeze over the lemon juice to avoid discolouration and set aside.

Whisk together the eggs and sugar in a large bowl until light and fluffy. Add the butter and whisk until well amalgamated. Split the vanilla pod with a sharp knife and scoop out the seeds with the tip of the knife, then add them to the bowl. Sift in the flour, then fold it in. Add and fold in the apples and lemon zest.

Pour the mixture into the prepared tin and bake for about 40 minutes, or until golden and springy to the touch. Remove from the oven and allow to cool in the tin. To serve, unmould from the tin and place on a serving plate. Slice and enjoy with tea or coffee.

CONSERVE

PRESERVES

Preserving food has always been important in my kitchen. It is a way of keeping the scents and flavours of produce long after it is in season. When I was a child, our store cupboard was always full of jars of preserved bell peppers, aubergines (eggplant), courgettes (zucchini), mushrooms, green beans, artichokes, giardiniera (mixed vegetables), tomatoes, cherries, peaches and various fruit jams. We made most preserves ourselves, but friends and neighbours would come round with gifts of their own preserved goodies too.

The end of summer was a busy time for us, as the family prepared for the preservation of the beloved tomatoes. Kilos and kilos of them had to be bottled in order to give us a year-long supply. As well as bottling them, we sun-dried them and made concentrato (a very thick tomato paste). On balconies and terraces throughout our village, trays of salted tomatoes that had been sliced in half were dried in the hot sun. For the concentrato, they were put through a mincer to extract the pulp, which was then put in large, flat, terracotta dishes, covered with nets to keep the flies off, and placed in the sun. The mixture had to be stirred every couple of hours with a large wooden spoon and sprinkled with a little olive oil to prevent a crust from forming. The dishes were taken in at night and brought out again in the early morning for about 3 days, until the pulp had turned into a thick, delicious concentrate of pure tomato. It was then transferred into jars, drizzled with a little olive oil and stored. Just a little of this pure nectar was needed to make the most amazing ragù sauce for Sunday lunch. Not even the best shop-bought variety will ever match the flavour.

We preserved throughout the year, but mainly during spring, summer and fall. Aubergines, peppers, green beans and artichokes were placed in oil so that we could enjoy them later as antipasto or as a snack with bread. Peaches and cherries were preserved in syrup or alcohol or made into jam; figs were sun-dried and eaten at Christmas, and strawberries and end-of-summer berries were made into delicious jam to be eaten on bread or in my mother's crostate (tarts). We preserved all sorts of vegetables in pure wine vinegar to make our own version of giadiniera (see page 224). The vinegar was always our own, made with leftover wine that was poured into a large glass container to which a couple of pieces of dried pasta would be added – this helped to speed up the process of turning the wine into vinegar. We would leave the container open for about 20 days, gently shaking it daily, until the wine turned into the most pungent vinegar. The vinegar was then transferred into smaller bottles and sealed with a cork. I still do this at home today.

My mother even preserved her own tuna. When the fishermen caught this fish, word would spread around the village very quickly and housewives would assemble on the beach to buy pieces just for preserving. It involved a lengthy process of gently cooking the fish in salty water and then drying it, before placing it in jars with olive oil. The results were worthwhile and my mother made lots to keep in our store cupboard for quick, healthy meals. Families also preserved their own anchovies and sardines. A few years ago, when I was on holiday on the Sicilian island of Lipari, I preserved some anchovies and brought them home to enjoy at Christmas – the taste was amazing and reminded us of being back on the sunny island.

Preserving food doesn't just lock away its freshness; as you enjoy it, memories of where you were when you ate it, what time of year it was, who you were with and, maybe, even what you were talking or thinking about while you were doing the preserving will flood back.

We now find all sorts of produce all year round, but I still like to preserve. During autumn when we go mushroom-picking, and I love to preserve porcini (ceps) or chiodini (honeyfungus), which we enjoy having with our Christmas lunch antipasto, as well as giving away as presents. Liz's favourite is preserved aubergines and peppers, which again we enjoy as antipasto. My friend Paolo also loves to preserve, and at the end of summer, when his allotment flourishes, he comes bearing gifts of delicious fruit jams and mixed pickle. I hope this tradition does not die away; I certainly keep it alive and hope my young daughters will do the same when they are older.

Preserving basics

- Always use very fresh, good-quality fruit and vegetables that are in season.

- To sterilize jars: wash and thoroughly clean all the jars you are going to use, then rinse out with a little white wine vinegar. Leave to drain, then dry well. If you are using new jars, after washing them place in a large pan of boiling water and boil for a couple of minutes. Remove, drain and dry well.

- To pasteurize: once you have placed the preserves in jars, seal well, preferably using hermetically sealed lids. Wrap each jar in old kitchen cloths – this prevents it from breaking during boiling. Line a large pan with kitchen cloth. Place the wrapped jars in it and add enough cold water to cover them by 3cm/1 inch. Bring the water to the boil, then reduce the heat to medium and boil for the time stated in the recipe. Turn off the heat, but leave the jars in the water until it is cold. Remove the jars and unwrap, then dry with a clean cloth, label and place in the store cupboard.

MAKES 12 PEPPERS IN A TALL 2 LITRE/
3¹/₂ PINT/8-CUP JAR

12 long, thin, sweet green (bell)
peppers, about 350g/12oz in total

400ml/14fl oz/1³/₄ cups white wine
vinegar or preserving vinegar

20 black peppercorns

6 bay leaves

1 litre/1³/₄ pint/4 cups olive oil
or good sunflower oil

for the filling

150–160g/5¹/₂ oz canned tuna in oil,
drained (keeping a little oil aside)

20g/³/₄oz capers, finely chopped

9 anchovy fillets in oil, drained
and finely chopped

Peperoni dolci ripieni sott'olio

Preserved filled sweet peppers

I love these long, thin, sweet green peppers, known as *friggitelli* in Campania. I usually buy them in Greek or Turkish shops and find they are slightly larger than the Italian ones; however, the sweet, delicate taste is similar and they are ideal for stuffing. When I find them, I buy lots, fill them with tuna and preserve them in oil so I can enjoy them as picked, as a little antipasto or light meal with bread. In Italy, my mother would fill and preserve tiny bell peppers at the end of summer.

Sterilize jars with a total volume of 2 litres/3¹/₂ pints/ 8 cups (see page 221) and dry thoroughly with a clean tea towel.

Using a small sharp knife, make a slit lengthways down one side of each pepper, then carefully remove the seeds and any white bits.

Place the vinegar in a pan and bring to the boil, then add a few peppers at a time and boil for 2 minutes, turning them over halfway through. Drain and leave to dry on kitchen towel.

Meanwhile, combine all the ingredients for the filling, adding a little of the tuna oil if necessary for binding.

Fill the peppers and place in the sterilized jars. Drop in the peppercorns and bay leaves and pour in the oil, making sure the peppers are covered. Secure with a vinegar-proof lid, and pasteurize for 30 minutes (see page 221). Label and store in a cool, dark, dry place for about 1 month before using. Once opened, store in the fridge.

Giardiniera

Mixed vegetable pickle

- - - -- - -- - - - - -- - -- - -- - - -- -

MAKES ABOUT 2 X 450ML/16FL OZ/1¾-CUP JARS

250ml/9fl oz/ generous 1 cup white
wine vinegar

12 black peppercorns

2 cloves

4 bay leaves

1½ tsp salt

2 carrots, cut into chunks

1 celery heart, cut into chunks

140g/5oz cauliflower florets

125g/4½oz green beans, topped and
tailed and halved

1 small red (bell) pepper, deseeded and
cut into thin strips lengthways

1 small yellow (bell) pepper, deseeded
and cut into thin strips lengthways

140g/5oz baby (pearl) onions, peeled

140g/5oz aubergine (eggplant),
peeled and cut into strips

85g/3oz green olives, pitted and halved

½ tsp dried oregano

4 red chillies (chiles), left whole

350ml/12fl oz/1½ cups olive oil, plus extra
to top up if necessary

- - - - -- - - - -- - - - -- - -- - - -- -

Giardiniera is a classic Italian mixed vegetable pickle. It was traditionally made by farmers using the season's new vegetables. In many families it was traditional to fill a large *tinozza* (wooden container) with wine vinegar, and each day put in whatever vegetable you could find. The vinegar preserved them and we enjoyed them as pickled vegetables throughout the winter. At home, my mother would religiously make jars of *giardiniera* at the end of summer, which we would use to enhance the famous *rinforzo* (cauliflower) salad at Christmas.

Sterilize 2 x 450ml/16fl oz/1¾-cup jars (see page 221) and dry thoroughly with a clean tea towel.

Put 250ml/9fl oz/generous 1 cup water into a large pan and add the vinegar, peppercorns, cloves, bay leaves and salt. Bring to the boil. Add the carrots, celery and cauliflower, lower the heat slightly and simmer for 10 minutes. Remove with a slotted spoon and place on a clean tea towel to cool.

Add the green beans to the vinegar solution and cook for 4 minutes, then remove and leave to cool on the tea towel.

Add the peppers and onions and cook for 3 minutes, then transfer to the tea towel. Finally, add the aubergine and cook for 1 minute. Remove and leave all the vegetables to dry out and cool.

Put all the vegetables in a large bowl, add the olives, oregano, chillies and olive oil and mix. Leave to infuse for a couple of minutes, then carefully, without breaking the vegetables, fill the sterilized jars, pressing gently down with your fingers so the olive oil covers all the vegetables. Leave to rest for a minute and, if necessary, add some more oil. Seal with vinegar-proof lids and pasteurize for 30 minutes (see page 221). Leave to cool, then label and store in a cool, dry, dark cupboard for about 1 week before using. Once opened, store in the fridge.

MAKES 1 X 400ML/14FL OZ/
1³/4-CUP JAR

2 large aubergines (eggplant), about
900g/2lb total weight

salt

700ml/1¹/4 pints/2³/4 cups white wine
vinegar or preserving vinegar

300ml/10fl oz/1¹/4 cups olive oil or
good sunflower oil, plus a little extra if
necessary to top up

2 garlic cloves, thinly sliced

¹/2 large red chilli (chile), thinly sliced

2 tsp dried oregano

Melanzane sott'olio

Preserved aubergines

My family loves this tasty way of preserving aubergines (eggplant). My wife Liz always makes a large quantity to be enjoyed at Christmas with our antipasto of cured meats. Everyone who tries them wants the recipe. My pregnant daughter-in-law, Judith, phoned one evening for the recipe in desperation to satisfy her craving! They really are tasty and make a delicious midnight snack on good country bread.

Sterilize a 400ml/14fl oz/1³/4-cup jars (see page 221) and dry thoroughly with a clean tea towel.

Peel the aubergines and cut lengthways into thin strips. Line a plastic container with the aubergine strips, sprinkle with a good handful of salt, then continue layering the aubergine and salt. Cover with greaseproof paper, place a weight on top and leave for 1 hour. During this time, the aubergines will exude quite a bit of water. Squeeze out the excess liquid, return to the container and cover with the vinegar, then with the clingfilm. Leave for a further 1 hour.

Drain the aubergines, squeezing out the excess vinegar with your hands. Place in a bowl with the oil, garlic, chilli and oregano and mix well, then fill the sterilized jar. Pack the aubergines snugly and, if necessary, top up with a little more oil. Secure with a vinegar-proof lid and, if you wish to keep them for some time, pasteurize for 20 minutes (see page 221). Otherwise, label and place in a cool, dry place for about 3 days before consuming. Once opened, store in the fridge.

Pomodori conservati a casa

Preserved tomatoes

MAKES ABOUT 4 X 500ML/18FL OZ/GENEROUS 2-CUP JARS

1.5kg/3lb 5oz tomatoes, preferably San Marzano or small plum tomatoes
a large handful of fresh basil leaves

Preserving tomatoes was an annual family ritual when I was a child – in fact, most people in our village would do it at the end of summer, when the local San Marzano tomato was plentiful. Lengthy preparations were made for it. I helped with gathering empty beer bottles and corks; a large table was set up in the garden with chairs around it for the production line to begin, and a big old oil drum was placed over a fire for the pasteurization process. We would preserve enough tomatoes to give us a year-long supply. Sometimes, when I'm lucky enough to get a glut of plum tomatoes at the end of summer, I like to carry on the tradition – of course, not in such a big way, but if I can get a dozen or so jars in my store cupboard, I'm happy.

Sterilize 4 x 500ml/18fl oz/generous 2-cup jars (see page 221) and dry thoroughly with a clean tea towel.

Halve or quarter the tomatoes (depending on their size) and use them to fill the jars, adding the odd basil leaf here and there. As you do this, gently press the tomatoes down and pack them in. Seal with the lids and pasteurize for 30 minutes (see page 221)., then remove them from the pan, leave to cool, then label and store in a dark, dry cupboard. Once opened, store in the fridge.

Pesche sciroppate

Peaches in syrup

During summer, when peaches were plentiful, our family friend, Maria Gatto, who lived in the hills above Minori, would always preserve them. Her vast garden was full of fruit trees, vegetables and herbs – produce she would use in her cooking. She was always cooking for her elderly husband and 6 children. She would spend entire days in her kitchen and work late into the night to create wonderful recipes and make pots and pots of delicious preserves. Whenever my mother went to see her, she would return home laden with jars of Maria's specialities. We would enjoy her peaches later in the year, when they were no longer in season, and use them in cakes or simply enjoy them in their lovely syrup.

Sterilize 4 x 400ml/14fl oz/1¾-cup jars (see page 221) and dry thoroughly with a clean tea towel.

Put the peaches into a bowl with the lemon juice and set aside.

Heat 500ml/18fl oz/generous 2 cups water in a saucepan with the sugar. Remove from the heat and leave to cool.

Drain the peaches and use them to fill the sterilized jars. Pour the cooled syrup over them, making sure you cover them completely. Secure with the lids.

Pasteurize for 1 minute (see page 221), then remove from the pan and leave to cool. Label and store in a cool, dry, dark cupboard until required. Once opened, store in the fridge.

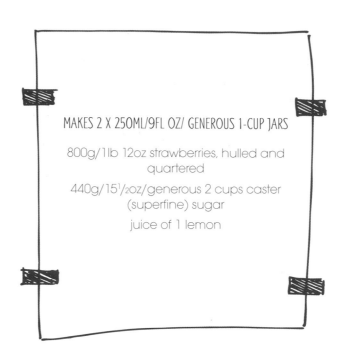

MAKES 2 X 250ML/9FL OZ/ GENEROUS 1-CUP JARS

800g/1lb 12oz strawberries, hulled and quartered

440g/15½oz/generous 2 cups caster (superfine) sugar

juice of 1 lemon

Marmellata di fragole

Strawberry jam

This is my mum's strawberry jam, which she made each year in May when strawberries were plentiful. I would collect the small wild strawberries, *fragoline*, that covered the hills above Minori. I had to resist eating too many of them on the way home because if I didn't bring enough my mum wouldn't make her delicious jam. I loved to watch her make it and was sometimes allowed to stir it, but the best treat of all was that she always let me have some of it warm on bread to test. Once potted, the jam was stored in the cupboard and she would use it to fill her delicious *crostata* (see page 210). This is a really simple recipe, made in no time, and so much better and more nutritious than any shop-bought variety.

Sterilize 2 x 250ml/9fl oz/generous 1-cup jars (see page 221) and dry thoroughly with a clean tea towel. Put a saucer in the freezer, for testing the jam later.

Place all the ingredients in a saucepan, bring to the boil and simmer on a medium heat for 20–30 minutes, stirring from time to time. To test if the jam is ready, place a little on a cold saucer – if it sets, it is ready.

Remove from the heat, fill the sterilized jars and seal with the lids. Pasteurize for 30 minutes (see page 221), Immediately place upside-down until cool. label and store in a cool, dry place and use when required. Once opened, store in the fridge.

MAKES 5 X 500ML/18FL OZ/GENEROUS 2-CUP
JARS

1.5kg/3lb 5oz damsons

300g/10$\frac{1}{2}$oz/1$\frac{1}{2}$ cups caster
(superfine) or granulated sugar

5 cloves

2 bay leaves

700ml/1$\frac{1}{4}$ pints/2$\frac{3}{4}$ cups pure grain
alcohol (available from good
Italian delis)

Susine selvatiche sotto spirito

Damsons in alcohol

I was in the country with my friend Paolo, cutting branches for my walking sticks, when we spotted a tree full of damsons. Of course, we had to pick them and, once home, I decided to preserve them in alcohol like we used to do in Italy. With his share, Paolo made jam, which we now enjoy with toast for our breakfast.

Sterilize 5 x 500ml/18fl oz/generous 2-cup jars (see page 221) and dry thoroughly with a clean tea towel.

Prick the damsons all over with a pin and set aside. Place 350ml/12fl oz/1$\frac{1}{2}$ cups water in a saucepan with the sugar, cloves and bay leaves. Cook over a medium heat until the sugar has dissolved. Remove from the heat and stir in the alcohol.

Fill the sterilized jars with the damsons, pour the liquid over them, making sure you cover them completely, and leave for a couple of minutes until the bubbles subside. Secure with the lids, label and leave for 3 months in a cool, dry, dark place before using. Once opened, store in the fridge.

MAKES 2 X 500ML/18FL OZ/
GENEROUS 2-CUP JARS

500g/1lb 2oz good cherries

225g/8oz/generous 1 cup caster
(superfine) or granulated sugar

300ml/10fl oz/1¹/₄ cups pure grain
alcohol (available from good
Italian delis)

Ciliegie sotto spirito

Cherries preserved in alcohol

Cherries are the first hint that summer really is on its way! I always look forward to seeing the trees in full bloom and the market stalls being piled high with the succulent fruit. Every year my father preserved cherries in alcohol so we could enjoy them later in the winter months. I do the same and look forward to opening a jar around Christmas time and enjoying a little taste of summer with a slice of cake.

Sterilize 2 x 500ml/18fl oz/2-cup jars (see page 221) and dry thoroughly with a clean tea towel. Put a saucer in the freezer, for testing the jam later.

Trim the cherry stems, leaving on about a quarter of their length. Prick the cherries all over with a pin.

Place 300ml/10fl oz/1¹/₄ cups water in a saucepan with the sugar. Put over a medium heat and stir until the sugar has dissolved. Remove from the heat and stir in the alcohol.

Fill the sterilized jars with the cherries and pour in the liquid, making sure you cover them completelly. Leave to cool, then secure with the lids and label. Leave for about 3 months in a cool, dry, dark place before using. Once opened, store in the fridge.

Index

ACKNOWLEDGEMENTS

Liz Przybylski for ghostwriting the book and organising me. Adriana for testing the recipes and cooking at the photo shoots. David Loftus for the outstanding photographs. Sara Mulvanny for the gorgeous illustrations. Georgina Hewitt for the art direction and design and Miranda Harvey for laying it all out. Paolo Baietti for helping at the photo shoots. Barbara for editing and correcting. Becca Spry at Pavilion for overseeing the project. Chloe, Olivia, Eoin Dylan and Freddie for being fabulous at the shoot. Luigi Bonomi, my agent.